By

Thomas L. Hodge

B.A. Psychology

M.A. Psychology

Table of Contents

For those who find there way

For those who lose it

For those who look for a way back

Introduction

Throughout the course of life, an individual develops various beliefs as the results of conflicts that they experience during developmental stages in life. An individual develops according to the events that occur during these stages of development. In a healthy situation, the individual will achieve a level of equilibrium and healthy understanding of the conflict that occurs during the critical stages of development. In an unhealthy situation, the individual will focus on the extreme resolutions of the conflict that will often provide for an unresolved situation or maladaptive resolution for the individual.

From these resolutions, the individual develops beliefs as to what is important in his or her life and a view of how he or she stands in the context of society and his or her environment. These beliefs affect the manner in which the individual understands the purpose and meaning for new experience and occurrences in life. The individual may develop dysfunctional beliefs based on the manner in which he or she handled crises in the development stages of life. In addition, a current or previous stage of life could cause the individual to develop irrational ideas about the meaning or purpose for what he or she is currently experiencing in life.

In understanding the process of how

dysfunctional thought processes develop and are maintained by an individual, treatment should focus on addressing not one area of dysfunction but addressing all three aspects of the process. This would include conscious raising techniques concerning the development, belief system, and meaning. The maladaptive development experience would be address through confronting the issue, address its presence, and attempting to put the issue behind the patient once resolved. Clear reasoning similar to REBT could restructure the belief system of the individual. Logotherapy coupled with the logical reasoning of REBT would assist the individual in gaining a better understanding of meaning. The three-pronged treatment would help to restructure the individual's understanding of the past, present, and future in a productive and healthy manner. Through this approach, an individual can confront an issue, overcome the issue, and understand that the changes he or she experiences will make them a better person in the end.

Personality Development

     To improve the quality of life of a person in a lasting manner, one will need to undo the psychological fortune that the person has experienced throughout life. To do this, the crises that the individual has experienced and how the affected his view on life must be brought to the surface. A person does not develop his understanding of the world in vacuum shut off from his environment. His interactions with family, friends, strangers, and other individuals shape the individual. The concept of self and interactions with the world are developed over time through conflicts that occur at different stages in life (Lachmann, 2004).

To explain development of an individual in society, the psychosocial stage theory provides a structured and chronological view of this development. In examining development through the eight psychosocial stages, a failure in one stage creates impairment as an individual goes through the proceeding stages and crises (Atalay, 2007). For example, an individual who experiences frustrations in the first stage would experience difficulties in sixth stage. If the person does not develop the ability to trust successfully in the first stage, he would not able to trust his partner enough during the sixth stage to be intimate with them. Similarly, a person who has been stagnate in early might experience despair in a later stage which would lead to depression.

In consideration of the individual's development, the stage with which the individual is currently struggling could be affected by a number of previous stages in combination or a single stage. For example, depression that is experience by an individual in the ego integrity versus despair stage could be experiencing the depression from unresolved issues with the intimacy stage if it deals with past failed relationships or the generativity stage if the concern is regarding life accomplishments. In addition, maladaptive experiences during the trust stage could be affecting the individual's willingness to trust his own judgment regarding his own life (Korte, Bohlmeijer,

Cappeliez, Smit, and Westerhof, 2012). In addition to elderly clients, a review of an individual's life is also useful in determining maladaptive experiences with a variety of age groups. For example, an individual that is struggling with the industry stage may have also experienced difficulty in the autonomy stage that is causing them to anxious about attempting to do things on their own. When examining individual's past, development in youth is given prevalence in the psychosocial stage theory as opposed to being marginalized. Regardless of the length of life that has been experienced, a great deal can be realized when that life is examined (Douvan, 1997).

Changing the Maladaptive Process

As the individual begins to understand of the dysfunctional perspectives that have developed over the course of his life, one should address the ways that the maladaptive process can be changed or coped with to improve the life of the individual. Cognitive approaches can advance the process of changing the perspective of the individual to reduce the effects of the frustrations or failures during the earlier and current stages of psychosocial development. Rational emotive behavior therapy serves as a useful approach in disrupting irrational belief systems. REBT effectively produces two different types of change in the individual. The first type of change is a change in a specific philosophy of a person's thought. The second type of change is a change is a general change of how an individual functions psychologically (Dryden and David, 2008). In confronting the reasoning and connections that have developed to create specific irrational philosophies, unhealthy beliefs can be distinguish from unhealthy beliefs. Through reviewing the development and history of the individual to the current beliefs, the therapist can direct the client in ways that they could rationalize or reformulate their understanding of the crisis.

During the process of disrupting irrational thoughts, the impairments that client has come to realize he or she is being affected by from prior crisis should be attended to frequently. For example, a client that is struggling with developing relationships may need to revert his attention back to trust issues frequently to understand some of the rational concerning his intimacy stage. As therapy proceeds, one may think that an early frustration or failure may be resolved, but the resolution of that early stage may need to be revisited. Years of reinforcement of irrational ideas take a great deal of effort to unlearn or inhibit. The human irrationality is often stronger than learning new information over a relatively short period (Dryden and David, 2008). It is, therefore, essential to reiterate an earlier change for the purpose of maintenance of past therapeutic experiences.

To address the past problems rationally, the client should step back and attempt to gain a new perspective. This new perspective is one of logic and reasoning. To aid the client in doing so, the therapist will maintain a genuine and authentic relationship with the client. In being authentic with the client, the therapist is able to bring reasoning into the interaction between the therapist and client (Still, 2006). The therapist does not further the irrational beliefs and ideas that the client has developed through his maladaptive experiences. The therapist leads the client down a new pathway of reason and clear thinking. The failures of past crises will be examined in a way that will turn the experiences from those that are impairments to experiences that allow the client to learn and adjust their behavior.

In addressing the failures of past crises, client should maintain an unconditional self-acceptance. The past experiences and shortcomings are in the past. There is nothing that can be fully done to change what had happened. However, the present and future can be changed, and the individual will need to accept themselves in the present and going forward (Elis, 2005). The idea of disregarding the past may seem to be counterproductive to examining the past, but the two processes combine to produce highly effective means of changing the present. One examines the past to learn from the mistakes that he or she has made and to realize the way in which the individual approaches a situation. The individual is, therefore, aware of the manner in which they would typically approach the issue and the maladaptive manner they are accustomed to behaving. With this understanding, the individual can rationally examine his or her behavior. In rationally examining the behavior, the individual can develop a new and healthier manner of thinking. This new healthy manner of thinking is the product of change.

Hedonistic Lifestyle

To create an effect that produces effects that impact not only the problem of initial focus but also other areas of life, this approach encourages the client to live a hedonistic lifestyle. The lifestyle is not hedonistic in short-term sense but in a long-term manner. Long-term hedonism focus on behaviors and thought process that benefit the individual over a longer period of time as opposed to a short-term pleasure that is unbeneficial. Through the process of long-term hedonism, the individual will experience high frustration tolerance and a continued acceptance of what happens throughout life (Ellis, 2005). The focus on long-term pleasure increases the quality of life for the individual. Other therapies often focus on only the reduction of problematic symptoms. Such treatments resolve the specific issue by short-term manipulation of the symptoms to create the illusion of an improved condition for the client. In doing so, a short-term solution will only delay the occurrence of the symptom's presentation or the root cause of the problem will manifest in a different manner. The belief or root cause of the issue is still maintained.

Encouraging long-term pleasure seeking, the individual will restructure his or her belief system and tendencies in a manner that is healthy and consistent with long-term solutions to the root cause of the problem.

For example, a patient may stop presenting suicidal tendencies and behaviors that were the consequence of a dissolved relationship as the result of a short-term solution, but he may still enter into his next relationship with the same underlying beliefs and psychological impairments that led to his suicidal ideations from the previous experience. A long-term hedonistic approach would address the underlying beliefs that led the individual down the mental pathway to suicidal ideations. This change would not only affect his thoughts about the current relationship but also future relationships as well. The individual would enter into new future relationships with a different mindset that would be healthy regardless of whether the relationship last forever or came to an end. Restructuring the beliefs of the individual creates long-term pleasure and solutions to a wide variety of problems the individual may experience by providing him with better tools to handle difficult situations (Ellis, Shaughnessy, and Mahan, 2002).

Meaning for Continuing

A dysfunctional development or changes in life lead to a dysfunctional view of meaning and purpose for an individual. A dysfunctional view of meaning appears as a common thread across several psychological disorders including depression, anxiety, eating disorders, and obsessive-compulsive disorders (Das, 1998a). An examination of how irrational beliefs effect an individual's perception of meaning can explain how that numerous individuals fall into a state of psychological dysfunction.

Providing the individual with meaning may serve to aid in advancing the changes set forth by evaluating the past and changing the beliefs of the individual. For example, studies have shown that elderly widows had grasp on their meaning for life as the result of the loss of spouses later in life (Koren and Lowenstein, 2008). In this case, the client could have developed a dysfunctional identity during the earlier stages of life as the result of tying their definition of who they are to the role that they played as a spouse. This could have some grounding in several stages. The individual could have developed doubt about himself or herself during the autonomy versus shame and doubt stage. The individual have long-seated inferiority issues about himself or herself. In addition, the role confusion may developed during adolescence or early adulthood that caused the individual to stop considering himself or herself an individual that is capable of functioning in a manner that is separate from the role of husband or wife of their deceased partner. The early dysfunctional experiences led to the beliefs that the individual developed about who he was and how he was to interact with society based on the roles he played. These beliefs led to a definition of meaning and purpose. When the spouse died, the individual ceased to have a purpose based upon the beliefs that he had developed over his lifetime.

In treating for meaning, one would address the individual's lack of self-identity. The client would review the events that they considered to be joint ventures of the past that involved the client assuming the role of that they had become entwined with as part of their definition of who they are. In considering the events of the past, the client would separate what behaviors and patterns of thought were the result of the role that they played and which behaviors and patterns were the result of the individual's unique self that was separate from the role they played. Examining the issue existentially, the existential void is a state of unknown that had been created by the individual's irrational beliefs about changing future and present experiences in a way that would make the experiences different from the past experiences that the individual has based their understanding and current maladaptive beliefs.

To provide the client with meaning for

the new beliefs, the client will be more accepting of the new philosophy. The new meaning would need to be supportive and congruent with the new philosophy in order to support the new rational beliefs that have replaced the prior irrational beliefs of the individual. The new meaning and belief that the client is directed toward should be supportive of a fulfilled existence for the individual. The new meaning will provide the client with a new role of being one's true self, acceptance of himself or herself as good, an understanding that they are different and unique from others, and a purpose for continuing forward in life toward new and unknown events (Längle, 2005). Once these four conditions are provided in the beliefs and meaning of the individual, the client will experience a fulfilled existence going forward.

One may consider that meaning has therapeutic purposes only for older clients who are struggling with the later stages of life who have lost a meaning for life due to fixations on maladaptive beliefs. Meaning and purpose is essential for all individuals. A young adolescent may believe that he must go to school in order to get good grades, but if there is no purpose or meaning for the individual to have good grades then the belief is irrelevant to influencing him to attend school. Finding meaning is essential for the young who are in search of meaning, the individual recovering from addiction, the elderly who have lost meaning, and the individuals who suffer from border, depression, anxiety, or an array of other mental illnesses (Das, 1998b). If individuals are provided meaning along with an understanding of their irrational beliefs and how the beliefs developed, the therapeutic process will have a more lasting effect.

Confronting the Issue

To improve life for the individual, more must be done than to simply understand that there is a problem. Based upon the three tenets of this approach, the individual has developed a thorough understanding of the problem that he or she is experiencing. From examining the individual life retrospectively, the individual understands how the maladaptive view was developed during past and present crises during the stages of development. From rationally reasoning through the individual's belief system, the individual understands how that they are creating the discomfort based on irrational beliefs that are illogically grounded. Through an exploration of meaning and purpose, the individual has examined and understood that his or her meaning in life can be adjusted to be more conducive to the new philosophy of how his or her life will be after changing the belief system from an unhealthy to a healthy system. Still the individual must confront the problem and produce change in his or her life.

Up to the point of confrontation, the individual has been provided with an array of tools to survive the confrontation with the problem. There comes a point at which the individual must address the issue with himself. This is not an easy task for the client. The individual will have to come to terms with his past first and realize that the past cannot be changed as it has already occurred. The mistakes of the past can be learned from but not dwelt upon for an improved quality of life. The past will be accepted for what it is and was and nothing more. The therapist may ask if the client feels as if he or she is the same person as the one who experienced the mistakes of the past. This may take some guiding and reasoning through open-ended questions to get the client to realize that they are different and can be different. By this point, a new philosophy about the client's beliefs will have been explored and developed. The client will confront the problem in a different manner than prior experiences.

Prior to therapy, the client might have

experienced hopelessness, fear, or panic as the result of confronting the event or reasoning that produced such dysfunctional emotions and irrationalities. The client will now confront the problem in a prepared manner. He will understand that he will overcome the problem and be a better person in the end.

While confronting and acknowledging the problem, the client will also acknowledge the change. The individual will confront the problem and come to determine that he will change his outlook and meaning in way that makes the problem no longer matter. The individual may also determine that the problem is still present in his life and acknowledge its presence, but he may determine that the problem is one that he is able to still exist bearing. He may also finding meaning and purpose in the suffering in that the problem has caused him; however, with a better understanding of the irrational and rational aspects of his beliefs, the individual will be better able to cope with the issues created by the problem. For example, a man was grieving over the loss of his wife. This caused him great sadness and depression that affected his daily functioning. After considering the circumstances, he found meaning in his suffering of having to live without her because his suffering resulted his bearing of the burden of out-living his wife so that she would not have to experience the sorrow and loss that he was going to upon her passing. By changing his perspective, the man found meaning in his grief, and his suffering was much more easier to cope with even though it was present because he had given meaning to his situation and changed his perspective (Frankl, 1963).

This confrontation has been referred to by a variety of names in different approaches, but the event is that which produces the change. Existentialists refer to it as kairos. Psychoanalysts refer to the moment in which the client gains insight while working through an issue. Cognitive therapists consider the change the moment when the irrational thoughts are disrupted and a new philosophy is accepted. Since psychosocial logotherapy is a combination of all three aspects, this moment is simply the moment of change. The client will not be facing a problem from only one angle and hoping that the angle of approach is effective enough to break down or break through the problem. The individual will be surrounding the problem and confronting the memories of the past and maladaptive developments in his life, the present beliefs that torment him daily, and the concerns about the future direction that the problem is affecting with regards to his meaning. Addressing the issue in this manner takes tears down the entire foundation of irrational thought and provides a new direction for the individual to have a better future.

Culture and Gender Sensitivities

The psychosocial development theory has often been noted as being applicable across cultures more so than other theories of development such as the Freudian psychosexual stages of development. The Eriksonian view of development has not only provided a clearer understanding of development but has also changed the way in which the dominant culture viewed development (Douvan, 1997). During the stages of development, one can note that cultural identity develops in a similar fashion through the same stages. Similarly, the psychosocial approach attempts to avoid a gender-bias so that it can maintain respect for the development of women as well as men.

When working with individuals of different cultures, genders, or sexual orientations, one should take efforts to understand the socially ascribed norms that are provided to individuals as they develop. These norms affect the perception and beliefs of the individuals. For example, an individual that has been raised in a communalistic culture is more likely to have a different definition of his identity than someone from an individualistic society. The person from the communalistic culture is more likely to identify with their family and neighbors than the person from non-communalistic culture. The beliefs of what is important to the person would also be affected by these cultural influences. In a communalistic culture, the person would be concerned more by the good of the group as opposed to his own self-advancement.

Factors such as these could have impacts on the interpersonal frustrations of people who are from different cultures. Some cultures discourage confrontation and conflict. In these cultures, a client may seem to be making changes; but in reality, the client might be only providing the therapists with the answers the therapists believes would be examples of change to avoid confrontation with the therapist. These types of beliefs would have a great impact on the direction of the therapeutic relationship.

In addition to the development and beliefs, the culture and gender of the client also has a great impact on the client's understanding of meaning and purpose. A female client in western society may have an easier time finding meaning in the role of being a mother and a wife as that is what the culture has told her that her role is. Since this is a role that she can relate to from what her culture has told her, she can easily find meaning in caring for her children in a manner that results in them being strong, independent, and successful. In Asian cultures, the woman may more easily find meaning in contributing to society by working and developing a successful career as opposed to a family.

One must consider the impacts of varying viewpoints upon the values and beliefs that fit into the formula that allows for understanding with this approach to therapy. The structure of therapy remains the same in that the individual develops through conflicts in stages, creates rational and irrational beliefs, and derives meaning and purpose based on those beliefs. The change is not to the structure of the therapy but to what seems irrational and maladaptive may seem logical and normal to the individual even more so due his or her culture and role in that culture. The key to overcoming such cultural barriers is for the client to realize that it is their choice to accept, reject, or question what their society and culture has provided them as definitions of what is normal. This process should occur concurrently through all aspects of the processes of examining development, confronting beliefs, and finding meaning.

Summary

The approach of psychosocial logotherapy provides a unique approach to treatment that focuses on improving the overall functioning of the individual. To accomplish this improvement, the approach attempts to produce change by addressing not only the dysfunction of the past or present, but it attempts to produce change by examining the past, the present and the future. People can learn a great deal from their past. The approach examines the past and the development of the individual through use of the psychosocial stages of development to understand how maladaptive behaviors and tendencies may have developed over time. The examination of the past raises the awareness of the individual to notice the patterns of their behaviors and the irrational instances that may have created such patterns of thought.

The approach takes note of the present by confronting the current beliefs that the individual is currently applying to his or her daily life. The therapist develops a relationship with the client that is built on trust by being authentic to allow for the therapist to aid the client in confronting, redirecting, and changing their systems of belief from irrational systems based on illogical connections to rational systems that are based on sound, logical judgment. In addition, the client modifies the current system of belief to focus upon increasing the degree of pleasure in a long-term mindset as opposed to a short-term focus. This long-term focus aids the individual in making healthy decisions.

Concerning the future, the approach provides meaning and purpose for that directs the decisions that are made based on the beliefs. This meaning reinforces the focus from the present and past portions of the therapy. As the client leaves therapy, the understanding of meaning aids to create a long-term solution for not only the initial problem that brought the client to therapy but also for other problems that may not have appeared. The emphasis on providing meaning to the client when coupled with the more rational belief system and the new understanding of his or her own development allows for the client to face new problems with the tools to resolve new issues and experience an improved quality of life.

Through this multi-faceted approach to treating the individual, the therapist can adapt the method as needed for differing cultures, genders, and sexual orientations. The approach attempts to reduce gender bias by considering elements that are essential to both men and women. In addition, the cultural flexibility of the approaches remains a strength of the approach when working with diverse groups of people. The final focus that remains connected between all groups is the connection between the past, present, and future of the individual and the way in which the improvement of the quality of life through psychological improvements is stressed throughout the therapeutic process.

References

Atalay, M. (2007). Psychology of Crisis: An Overall Account of the Psychology of Erikson. *Ekev Academic Review, 11*(33), 15-34.

Das, A. (1998a). Frankl and the realm of meaning. Journal of Humanistic Education & Development, 36(4), 199.

Das, A. (1998b). Frankl and the realm of meaning. *Journal of Humanistic Education & Development, 36*(4), 199.

Douvan, E. (1997). Erik Erikson: Critical times, critical theory. *Child Psychiatry & Human Development, 28*(1), 15-21.

Dryden, W., & David, D. (2008). Rational Emotive Behavior Therapy: Current Status. *Journal of Cognitive Psychotherapy*, 22(3), 195-209. doi:10.1891/0889-8391.22.3.195

Ellis, A. (2005). Why I (really) became a therapist. *Journal Of Clinical Psychology*, 61(8), 945-948. doi:10.1002/jclp.20166

Ellis, A., Shaughnessy, M. F., & Mahan, V. (2002). An Interview With Albert Ellis about Rational Emotive Behavior Therapy. *North American Journal Of Psychology*, 4(3), 355-366.

Frankl, V. (1963). *Man's Search for Meaning.* New York, NY: Washington Square Press.

Koren, C., & Lowenstein, A. (2008). Late-life Widowhood and Meaning in Life. Ageing International, 32(2), 140-155. doi:10.1007/s12126-008-9008-1

Korte, J., Bohlmeijer, E., Cappeliez, P., Smit, F., & Westerhof, G. (2012). Life review therapy for older adults with moderate depressive symptomatology: a pragmatic randomized controlled trial. *Psychological Medicine, 42*(6), 1163-1173. doi:10.1017/S0033291711002042

Längle, A. (2005). The Search for Meaning in Life and the Existential Fundamental Motivations. *Existential Analysis: Journal Of The Society For Existential Analysis, 16*(1), 2-14.

Lachmann, F. (2004). Identity and Self. *International Forum of Psychoanalysis, 13*(4), 246-253. doi:10.1080/08037060410004700

Still, A. (2006). Rationality and REBT. *Journal of Cognitive & Behavioral Psychotherapies*, 6(1), 5-10.